Professor Birdsong's 177 Dumbest Criminal Stories - International

Leonard Birdsong
Winghurst Publications

Professor Birdsong's 177 Dumbest Criminal Stories - International
by Leonard Birdsong
© 2015 Leonard Birdsong
ISBN: 978-0-9898452-3-6

Winghurst Publications
1969 S. Alafaya Trail / Suite 303
Orlando, FL 32828-8732
www.BirdsongsLaw.com
lbirdsong@barry.edu

Disclaimer:
The facts that are recounted in the stories in this volume are true and in the public domain, as best as Professor Birdsong can determine from his research of court documents, newspapers, and wire services. The author's commentaries on these stories are his own views and opinions and do not reflect the official policy or position of any Law school, Law firm or other organization with which the author may be affiliated. The opinions provided herein are not intended to malign or defame any religion, ethnic group, club, organization, company, individual or anyone or anything. The author further covenants and represents that the work contains no matter that will incite prejudice, amount to an invasion of privacy, be libelous, obscene or otherwise unlawful or which infringe upon any proprietary interest at common law, trademark, trade secret, patent or copyright. The author is the sole proprietor of the work and all parts thereof.

Permissions:
Cover graphic: ©TomasGriger|Dreamstime.com
                ©Ievgen Melamud|Dreamstime.com

Book cover design: Rik Feeney /
Rik@PublishingSuccessOnline.com

TABLE OF CONTENTS

INTRODUCTION

Professor Leonard Birdsong received his B.A. degree from Howard University and received his law degree from the Harvard Law School. After a rewarding career as a lawyer and diplomat he now lives in Orlando, Florida where he teaches Criminal Law, Evidence, and Immigration Law. He has written many scholarly legal articles since joining the legal academy. His latest scholarly piece is entitled: Reforming The Immigration Courts of the United States: Why Is There No Will To Make It An Article I Court?

This publication is not one of those scholarly pieces!

This volume of his *177 Dumbest Criminal Law Stories: International* is written just for fun and for your reading enjoyment. This volume should bring you many good laughs.

Professor Birdsong knows that it is good to get a good laugh at least once every day. That is why several years ago he began to collect and edit from the wire services and news the type of weird and funny criminal law stories about dumb criminals that appear in this volume.

Professor Birdsong wishes to thank his brilliant student research assistant, Arielle Lewis, for her editorial assistance on this volume. Facts and figures concerning a good number of the countries included in this volume were found at Country Profiles from:

http://www.cia.gov/library/publications/the-world-factbook/geos/ch.html.

You may find other volumes of Professor Birdsong's Dumbest Criminal Law Stories and his series of Weird Criminal Law Stories at Amazon.com, or by going to his website: LeonardBirdsong.com.

Enjoy!

CHAPTER ONE

Dumbest Criminals from China, Japan, and Vietnam

When many of you think of dumb criminal law stories, you may think they come just from the United States. But that's wrong. Feast your eyes herein on some of the dumbest international criminal law stories from China, Japan and Vietnam – all parts of the Far East.

CHINA

For centuries, China stood as a leading civilization, outpacing the rest of the world in the arts and sciences, but in the 19th and early 20th centuries, the country was beset by civil unrest, major famines, military defeats, and foreign occupation. After World War II, the communist under Mao Zedong established an autocratic socialist system that, while ensuring China's sovereignty, imposed strict controls over everyday life and cost the lives of tens of millions of people. After 1978, Mao's

7

successor Deng Xiaoping and other leaders focused on market-oriented economic development and by 2000 output had quadrupled. For much of the population, living standards have improved dramatically and room for personal choice has expanded, yet political controls remain tight. Since the early 1990's, China has increased its global outreach and participation in international organizations.

China's civil law has been influenced by the Soviet and continental European civil law systems.

The Chinese legislature retains power to interpret their statutes.

China's criminal procedure law was revised in early 2012.

China's chief of state is President Xi Jinping, since March 14, 2013.

Now, on to some of dumbest criminal law stories that have come out of China –

CHINA

CHINA: *Murder, by way of malicious gonad grabbing?* A woman has been accused of killing a man by squeezing his scrotum. The gonad attack came when the man complained to the woman about parking her motor scooter in front of his store. The argument got so heated that the woman grabbed the shopkeeper and yelled, "I'll squeeze it to death! You'll never have children again!" Her grip was so strong the man went into shock and died.

CHINA: *There is no such thing as a free lunch?* A Chinese man found that there is such a thing as a free lunch if one is willing to eat at the airport. The man managed to scam months' worth of free meals in the VIP lounge at Xi'an Airport in Shaanxi by buying a first-class ticket, and then switching his flight to the next day after he ate. The man continued to switch over and over until the ticket expired, when he simply cancelled it.

CHINA: *Yep – size does matter!* A Taiwanese woman divorced her husband because his penis was too small. The 52-year old bride learned the "little" truth on their wedding night. She also said he couldn't perform in several attempts, and had refused to seek treatment.

CHINA*: Sex slows.* Lin Chen, a 67-year-old woman who lives in Ningbo, who believed that police were not doing enough to stop speeding drivers on her street came up with a brilliant idea. She tied a blow up sex doll to a tree outside her house. This prompted drivers to slow down to gawk and wonder why. Police contend that since the doll went up, traffic accidents have gone down. Who knew?

CHINA: *Oh what a yucky mess that must have been....*Probably painful too... It has been reported that a Chinese man nearly died when he tried to win a beer chugging contest. He allegedly started feeling dizzy and sick to his stomach after swallowing his first two beers. When he tried to hold in the vomit, his esophagus exploded. We learn the man was treated at a local hospital.

CHINA: *The "meaning" is you are going to jail!* Another Chinese man loved knowledge so he was willing to steal for it. The man identified only as Mr. Lee, allegedly stole 800 books of poetry, science and history from a small town bookshop. When police found him with the merchandise, he said he pulled off the burglary in an effort to find "the meaning of life."

CHINA: *WOOF WOOF...SUCKERS!* A zoo in the city of Luohe has come under scrutiny after charging patrons to see a "lion" that turned out to be a dog in disguise. The dog was painted tan like a lion and given a fake mane. Zoo visitors became suspicious, however, after the "lion" started barking. The zoo was also accused of trying to pass off a disguised fox as a snow leopard.

CHINA: Police in Shanghai recently received hundreds of telephone calls from panicked citizens reporting unidentified flying objects buzzing the city. As it turns out, the UFO's were birthday cake delivery drones being used by a clever bakery shop owner looking to get some media attention. Come on! We now actually have birthday cake delivery drones in the skies! Ridiculous...

CHINA: *...By pig epidemic do they mean swine flu?* Chinese officials are probing why 900 pigs were floating dead in the Shanghai River. The river is the main water source for the massive Chinese city, making the discovery particularly disturbing for residents. One official said that there was no sign that the pigs were dumped or that there was a pig epidemic.

CHINA: *This sounds like an older man's fantasyland.* We learn that a retired couple was arrested after police figured out that the senior center they ran was actually a brothel. The facility in the southwestern city of Chongqing catered to men over sixty years old.

China's highest court is the Supreme people's Court which consists of over 340 judges, including the Chief Justice. The Chief Justice is appointed by the People's National Congress with terms limited to two consecutive 5-year terms.

CHINA: *Those dummies!* Sex dolls must be very popular in China. We learn that a team of 18 police officers in Shandong worked frantically to save a woman they thought was in distress in a river. Some 1,000 people gathered to watch the operation. They witnessed the embarrassed officers as they "rescued" an inflatable sex doll.

CHINA: *There's nothing like crazy, love sick kids getting naked and threatening to jump off* *a bridge in winter. Happens all the time...*We hear there was a lot of rubbernecking when a young couple whose parents were trying to keep them apart stripped naked and stood on a bridge in Guangzhou, embracing and threatening to jump. The cold weather cooled their ardor and they gave themselves up. A police spokesman said "Our biggest problem was blocking traffic so motorists didn't drive into each other trying to get a better look."

CHINA: *Oh yuck!* Security officials at a Guangzhou Airport stopped a South Korean passenger trying to carry a forbidden bottle of liquid onto a flight. They told her to drink her beverage or discard it. She drank the liquid but refused to swallow and when police made her spit into a bucket, they discovered dozens of tadpoles she was trying to sneak on board.

CHINA: *Wow, how ugly was that baby?* A father won a $120,000 lawsuit against his wife for giving birth to a daughter whom he called "horrifyingly" ugly. The man convinced a court that his wife tricked him by getting massive plastic surgery to look beautiful. He said he learned the truth only when the baby daughter wound up resembling the mom's old face. Perhaps, he can use the $120,000 to give the baby plastic surgery.

JAPAN

Japan attacked U.S. forces in 1941, triggering America's entry into World War II – and said war soon occupied much of the East and Southeast Asia. After its defeat in World War II, Japan recovered to become an economic power and an ally of the U.S. While the emperor retains his throne as a symbol of national unity, elected politicians hold actual decision-making power.

Following three decades of unprecedented growth, Japan's economy experienced a major slowdown starting in the 1990's, but the country remains a major economic power. In March 2011, Japan's strongest-ever earthquake, and an accompanying tsunami, devastated the northeast part of Honshu Island, killing thousands and damaging several nuclear power plants. The catastrophe hobbled the country's economy and its energy infrastructure, and tested its ability to deal with humanitarian disasters.

Japan's civil law system is based on the German model; their system also reflects Anglo-American influence and Japanese traditions.

The highest Japanese court is the Supreme Court or Saiko Saibansho which consists of the Chief Justice and 14 associate justices.

The chief of state is Emperor Akihito since January 7, 1989.

Now that you know these facts, here are some dumbest criminal stories from Japan—

JAPAN

JAPAN: *They describe him as homeless, but "well-heeled."* An unemployed Tokyo man with no permanent address kept 450 pairs of women's high heels that he had stolen in a rented room. Soho Shoso, 28 told police "I've felt pleasure in stealing high heels. I was not interested in brand new products."

JAPAN: *Surely a pervy weirdo...* A 38-year-old Tokyo police officer, who reportedly admitted to friends that he wanted to be a high school girl, was fired recently for allegedly dressing up in a sailor girl outfit and exposing himself to a 16 year old teen. The report indicates that the officer had previously been arrested for exposing himself in public.

JAPAN: *Meow!* A man on a yearlong burglary spree stole nearly $180,000 in cash and valuables to feed his 120 cats a gourmet diet, according to police. Mamoru Demizu, 48, of Izumi city is suspected of breaking into houses 32 times to provide the $250-a-day cat feast.

JAPAN: *The rise of the planet of the apes??* It has been reported that fifteen monkeys at a primate research center in Kyoto taught themselves to elude a 15 foot electrified fence by using tree branches to catapult themselves and escape one by one. Once they were over, however, the monkeys did not know what to do next, so they waited outside and were lured back in with food. *It has been said that "If you give 100 monkeys 100 typewriters, in 100 years at least one of those monkeys will write a novel."*

JAPAN: *What a "pisser."* A rail commuter was fined $12,000 after investigators concluded that he had been urinating in the Chihaya train station elevator every work day for six months. Officials contend the fine matched the cost of fixing the corroded elevator. The commuter challenged the fine, claiming that poor initial construction of the elevator resulted in the high cost of repairs.

JAPAN: *How big were the men?* Explosive boobs and butts sound very dangerous... Authorities say they have broken up a prostitution ring that specialized in home delivery of working girls weighing as much as 330 pounds. The service, called "Makusu Bod," was run by a heavyweight madam named Keiko Saito and promised to provide women to men who liked "explosives boobs and butts"

JAPAN: *Ah so*....A Japanese business owner has filed a lawsuit against the head of the country's Mafia, Kenichi Shinoda, and demanding return of protection money she paid him. The lady maintains that she paid $109,000 to the feared Yakuza boss. Shinoda once spent time in prison for chopping a rival in half with a Samurai sword. The lady might want to reconsider her suit.

VIETNAM

Under the Geneva Accords of 1954, Vietnam was divided into the communist North and the anti-communist South. U.S. economic and military aid to South Vietnam grew through the 1960's in an attempt to bolster the government, but U.S. armed forces were withdrawn following bloody fighting by U.S. forces and a cease-fire in 1973. Two years later, North Vietnamese forces overran the south reuniting the country under communist control. Since the enactment of Vietnam's renovation policy in 1986, Vietnamese authorities have committed to increased economic liberalization and enacted structural reforms needed to modernize the economy and to produce more competitive, export-driven industries.

The Vietnamese legal system is a civil law system that reflects a European-style system.

Vietnam's highest court is the Supreme People's Court which consists of a Chief Justice and 13 associate justices.

The head of state is President Truong Tan Sang since July 25, 2011.

Although Professor Birdsong has not travelled to or attended court in in China, Japan, Vietnam or other far eastern countries, it would be his advice to try to keep your nose clean when travelling in these countries. Try not to get into trouble and have to go to jail. Their legal systems are very convoluted and not like those here at home in the United States. Everything in these courts will be presented to you through a translator, if you are lucky!

VIETNAM

VIETNAM: *Hiss, Hiss times 53...* Police stopped a driver outside of Hanoi and found his car filled with 53 live king cobras. The venomous snakes were on their way to a restaurant, where they are served as a delicacy. The driver was arrested. But the worst part for him was that he was only paid $50 to haul the dangerous cargo.

VIETNAM: *Temper, temper!* A Vietnamese man learned the hard way he had better keep his temper in check. The man had become so enraged over a baby crying on a flight to Ho Chi Minh City that as soon as the plane landed and came to a stop, he pulled the escape chute and tried to slide out of the plane. Now he owes the airline $10,000. *Again, we caution temper: temper, temper.*

CHAPTER TWO

Dumbest Criminal Stories from Around the Indian Ocean Basin

European explorers began establishing footholds in the subcontinent of India during the 16th century. By the 19th century, Great Britain had become the dominant political power on the subcontinent. The British Indian Army played a vital role in both World Wars. Years of nonviolent resistance to British rule, led by Mahatma Gandhi and Jawaharlal Nehru, eventually resulted in Indian independence, which was granted in 1947. Large-scale communal violence took place before and after the subcontinent partition into two separate states – India and Pakistan.

The two neighboring nations have fought three wars since independence, the last of which was in 1971 and resulted in East Pakistan becoming the separate nation of Bangladesh. Despite pressing problems of overpopulation, excessive poverty environmental degradation, and widespread corruption, economic growth following the launch of economic reforms in 1991 and a massive youthful population are driving India's emergence as a regional and global democratic power.

Indian law is based on a common law system on the English model. There are separate personal law codes that apply to Muslims, Christians and Hindus.

The highest court is the Supreme Court.

The chief of state is President Pranab Mukherjee since July 22, 2012.

Here are a few dumbest criminal stories. These come from India and around the Indian Ocean Basin. They are really funny and weird.

INDIA

INDIA: *Weapons-grade spice! Who knew?* A group of criminals hijacked a train and freed a fellow gang member by using local hot chili powder. The bandits threw the powder in the faces of the police, freed their cohort and fled.

INDIA: *Apparently pachyderms and moonshine do not mix well.* A pack of drunken elephants tore through an Indian village after they got into 500 gallons of moonshine. The elephants destroyed 12 homes in Dumurkota, where police and villagers eventually herded the elephants back over a river and onto to their migration route.

INDIA: *Just make sure you spell Hitler correctly on the ballot!* Among the 345 candidates who had run for the national assembly in the latest election in India are Adolf Lu Hitler, Frankenstein Momin, Billy-Kid Sangma and Jhim Carter Sangma. "Parents get fascinated by names of well-known people but are unaware that some are infamous," said a local teacher. *You think?*

INDIA: *...Those would have been some mighty big "drones."* This one is about the Indian military. Radar-telescope soldiers had suspected for six months that Chinese "drones" were spying on them which lead to a diplomatic incident. Finally, military intelligence officials consulted the Indian Institute of Astrophysics – which determined that the "drones" were actually the planets Jupiter and Venus.

INDIA: *Dastardly grand pappy?* A greedy grandfather got caught after he sold his newborn grandson on Facebook for $830. The 47-year-old man told his daughter that the child had died. Police say two temp workers at the hospital helped the grandfather arrange the sale to a businessman in Delhi. Authorities arrested all three and are questioning the buyer. The baby is being kept safe with authorities.

INDIA: Police in New Delhi don't condone drunk driving, or even riding the subway when inebriated. As a result, police have set up Breathalyzers at metro stations entrances, with apparent tipsy riders being compelled to submit to blood-alcohol tests. Police say they are trying to prevent tragic train run overs. *If they are worried about run overs shouldn't they have also tested the subway drivers' blood-alcohol levels?*

AUSTRALIA

Prehistoric settlers arrived on the continent of Australia from Southeast Asia at least 40,000 years before Europeans began exploring. In 1770, British sea captain James Cook took possession of the east coast of Australia in the name of Great Britain. All of Australia was claimed as British territory in 1829 with the creation of the colony of Western Australia. Subsequently six colonies were created in the late 18th and 19th centuries; they federated and became the Commonwealth of Australia in 1901.

The new country took advantage of its natural resources to rapidly develop agricultural and manufacturing industries and to make major contribution to the Allied effort in World Wars I and II. In recent decades, Australia has become an internationally competitive, advanced market economy due in large part to economic reforms adopted in the 1980's and its location in one of the fastest growing regions of the world economy.

The Australian legal system is a common law system based on the English model.

The country's highest court is the High Court of Australia. The Chief of State of Australia is Queen Elizabeth II since February 6, 1952.

AUSTRALIA

AUSTRALIA: Two people landed in jail because of a tattoo needle. Three Aussie men, one of them a tattoo artist, got drunk one night earlier this year. The tattoo artist and his accomplice persuaded the third man to get some skin art. The man chose a yin-yang design, but when he woke up, he found a 15-inch penis inked on his body. *YOW!*

AUSTRALIA: A burglar in Brisbane got much more than he bargained for when he was confronted by the 83-year-old homeowner, Edwin Dowdy and his wife. The two of them are trained in the Japanese martial art of Aikido. Dowdy contends the muscular burglar ran into the senior citizen's knife, leaving the fleeing burglar with a serious stomach wound. *So Aikido has something to do with knife fighting?*

AUSTRALIA: *OUCH!* What kind of sex was he planning on having? A man ended up in the hospital emergency room where he surprised doctors when an X-ray found that he had stuck a fork into his penis. The man had hoped the utensil would serve as a sexual aid. However, since this did not work out doctors removed the fork with lubricant and forceps. *OUCH! OUCH!*

AUSTRALIA: *Just maybe, the thief needed something in which to dunk his cookies?* A man was arrested by police after stealing a tanker truck containing 5,811 gallons of milk. The 20-year-old thief led police on a two hour chase after the vehicle was stolen from the town of Maffra southeast of Melbourne, and was caught after police used spike strips.

AUSTRALIA: *He just wants more time away from those nine kids!* A father of nine sentenced to 13 years in prison after police seized his $70 million marijuana crop filed an appeal – because he says his prison stint is too short. Michael Gardner, 58, wearing a right-to-life T-shirt in court and, seemingly reveling in the publicity of the case, told the judge he had not been given proper recognition for the "full gravity" of his offense.

AUSTRALIA: *A policeman's work is never done!* A bold thief pulled a heist in a hotel in Hobart while hundreds of police officers were on the premises partying before the start of a law enforcement Aussie-rules football championship. The bandit made off with hundreds of dollars from a gaming room when a clerk left the cash register unattended for a moment. Red faced detectives are studying the surveillance video.

AUSTRALIA: *What a load of crap!* Australia has a strange new export – koala poop. It is very popular in Japan, where students believe it brings them luck on tests. That is because the cuddly-looking koalas are famous for being tenacious. They have been known to hang on trees for more than 20 hours at a time. Students who receive the product think it will inspire them to pull enough all-nighters to ensure success on college admission exams. *PHEW!*

AUSTRALIA: *YOW! HOT, HOT...CAN'T SEE...HELP.... OH LORDY...* The chili powder at the O'Le Portuguese restaurant in Sydney isn't just good, it's the ultimate weapon. When the chicken joint was robbed a few weeks ago, an employee didn't just helplessly stand by – instead, he fought off the crook by tossing a bucket of the eatery's famous chili flakes on him which acted like Mace.

AUSTRALIA: *Strange things happen in 7-Elevens.* A bandit wearing an overturned flower pot on his head and wielding a running chain saw entered a 7-Eleven in Flinders View, and demanded cash. He didn't get any money, but he did moon the staff, damaged displays and then fled.

NEW ZEALAND

The British colony of New Zealand became an independent dominion in 1907 and supported Britain militarily in both World Wars. New Zealand's full participation in a number of defense alliances lapsed in the 1980's.

The New Zealand legal system is a common law system, based on the English model.

The legal system is a common law system based on the English model.

The country's highest court is the Supreme Court.

The Chief of State is Queen Elizabeth II since February 6, 1952.

NEW ZEALAND: *What was he going to do with that*? A traveler got caught trying to smuggle a donkey penis into New Zealand. The smuggler arrived at the airport in Wellington and declared to customs he had food in his bag. Officials then found the foot-long equine phallus and they confiscated the illegal item.

NEW ZEALAND: *Was any of the money recovered??* New Zealand's "accidental millionaire" is now in jail. Gas station owner Hui Gao, 32, fled back to China in 2009 after a bank mistakenly deposited $8 million in his bank account. It took months for the opportunistic thief to be extradited, but now he has been sentenced to four years and seven months in prison.

SRI LANKA

SRI LANKA: *What a great record!!* We hear that if you're looking for one of the world's easiest jobs, the country of Sri Lanka is advertising to hire two hangmen. While Sri Lanka has 357 people on death row, the country has not actually executed anyone for 36 years.

The first Sinhalese arrived in Sri Lanka late in the 6th century B.C. from Northern India. The island was ceded from Portugal to the British in 1796, and became a crown colony of England in 1815. Formerly known as Ceylon, it became independent of Britain in 1948; its name was changed to Sri Lanka in 1972. Tensions between the Sinhalese majority and Tamil scenarists erupted into war in 1983. After two decades of fighting, the government and Liberation Tigers of Tamil Eelam formalized a cease-fire in February 2002 with Norway brokering peace negotiations. Violence between the government and the Tamil tigers intensified in 2006, but by May 2009 the government announced defeat of the scenarists. Since the end of the conflict the government has enacted an ambitious program of economic development.

The Sri Lankan legal system is a mixed legal system of Roman-Dutch civil law, English common law, and Jaffna Tamil customary law.

The country's highest court is the Supreme Court of the Republic.

The chief of state and head of the government of Sri Lankan is President Mahinda Percy Rajapaksa.

SRI LANKA: It's hard to make a call when you butt dial! Have you ever heard of "butt-dialing?" Read this: A 58-year –old convict had his forbidden cell phone between his rear end cheeks when a guard came by his cell. And then... the phone rang. The guard confiscated the cell phone. We hope he used latex gloves to make the extraction.

MAYLAYSIA

During the late 18th and 19th centuries, Britain established colonies and protectorates in the area of current Malaysia; these were occupied by Japan from 1942 to 1945. In 1948, the British-ruled territories on the Malay Peninsula, except Singapore, formed the Federation of Malaya, which became independent in 1957. Malaysia was formed in 1963 when the British colonies of Singapore joined the federation. Between 1981 and 2003, Malaysia was successful in diversifying its economy from dependence on exports of raw materials to the development of manufacturing, services and tourism.

The legal system of Malaysia is a mixed system of English common law, Islamic law, and customary law.

The country's highest court is the Federal Court.

The head of government is Prime Minister Mohamed Najib bin Tun Abdul Razak.

MAYLAYSIA: A teacher in Malaysia forced his students to eat grass as punishment for not doing their homework. The English language teacher also made some of the lazy children wear bells around their necks to shame them. After outraged parents complained, the teacher was transferred to a school with blacktop and no grass outside.

MAYLAYSIA: Cattle rustlers don't get away! Thieves in Malaysia stuffed three full-sized cows into a tiny Proton Wira automobile, which is about the size of a Toyota Corolla. They had taken out the back seats for more room, but they didn't get far, as the animals weighed them down. Police eventually caught up them and arrested them. *MOOOO...*

MALAYSIA: *Police are vowing to get to the bottom of a sexy mystery.* Three scantily clad transvestites who performed at a law-enforcement dinner were not the official entertainment, police insist. The transvestites allegedly crashed the party. Fat chance! More likely than not one of the police in charge of the entertainment had a crush on one of the trannies...We all know how it works in Malaysia.

MALAYSIA: *What great investigative police work!* Police in the capital of Kuala Lumpur said a car wash was offering free sex in a massage parlor to drivers who bought nine washes. Police learned about the special deal when they raided the parlor and found car wash cards on many of the patrons.

INDONESIA

The Dutch began to colonize Indonesia in the early 17th century. Japan occupied the islands from 1942 to 1945. Indonesia declared independence before Japan's surrender at the end of World War II. From 1967 until 1998 President Suharto ruled Indonesia. After rioting toppled Suharto in 1998, free and fair elections took place in 1999. Indonesia is now the world's third most populous democracy, the world's largest archipelagic state and the world's largest Muslim-majority nation.

Indonesia's civil law system is based on the Roman-Dutch model and is influenced by customary law.

The country's highest court is the Supreme Court of Mahkamah Agung

The chief of state and head of government is President Susilo Bambang Yudhoyono since October 20, 2004.

INDONESIA

INDONESIA: *The headline read: The Burglar might have been a Great Nanny."* A burglar broke into an Indonesian home with the intent to steal valuables. He tied up the married couple in order to rob them, but when their hungry baby started crying he warmed up baby formula and bottle fed the infant while rocking it in his arms. He eventually fled without taking values. Police soon captured him, but at least the infant went to sleep.

INDONESIA: Authorities here discovered 1,495 pig nosed turtles in two pieces of baggage heading out of the country. The turtles, considered an endangered species, can grow as heavy as 44 pounds and are a favorite of smugglers. Authorities surmise that the turtles were being transported for resale. *You think!!*

CHAPTER THREE

DUMBEST CRIMINALS STORIES FROM RUSSIA AND EASTERN EUROPE

Professor Birdsong has never been to Eastern Europe or Russia, but he has found some dumb criminal law stories from over there that you might enjoy.

Repeated devastating defeats of the Russian army in World War I led to widespread rioting in major cities of the Russian Empire and to the overthrow in 1917 of the imperial household. The communists under Vladimir Lenin seized power soon after and formed the USSR. Russia has shifted its post-soviet democratic ambitions in favor of a centralized semi-authoritarian state in which the leadership seeks to legitimize it rule through managed elections, populist appeals by president Putin, and continued economic growth.

The Russian legal system is a civil law system; there is judicial review of legislative acts.

The country's highest court is the Supreme Court of the Russian Federation.

The chief of state is President Vladimir Vladimirovich Putin since May 7, 2012.

RUSSIA

RUSSIA: *It was a Pussy Riot!* The Russian Supreme Court ordered a review of the case of two women from the band Pussy Riot, holding lower courts had failed to provide full evidence of their guilt and overlooking mitigating factors in sentencing them to two years in prison. The ruling may have meant shorter sentences for Nadezhda Tolokon-Nikova and Maria Alyokhina. Subsequently, during Christmas week, 2013 Vladimir Putin granted them amnesty and had them released from prison.

RUSSIA: We've learned that a former teacher in Yekaterinburg stabbed a man to death in a drunken argument about the merits of poetry versus prose. The stabber preferred poetry. *DUMB!*

RUSSIA: *...And that is why one should always read the fine print!* A clever Russian tired of credit card offers turned the tables on that country's online bank by drawing up his own credit card contract and slipping it past bank officials. Dmitry Agarkov, 42, scanned the bank's contract and doctored the fine print to give him unlimited credit, a "0" percent interest with no fees or penalties ever – and the bank signed off on the deal. The bank sued Agarkov for $1,363 in late charges, but a judge ruled in his favor that the bank had signed and agreed to a valid contract.

...And that is why one should always read the fine print!

RUSSIA: *There's nothing like being on the run with a hot fox!* He could not bear to part with his foxy lady – nope, make that his lady fox. An assistant fired from a Siberian circus is suspected of stealing a fox named Eva and has been seen walking her around on a leash. Gennady Pyatibratov, 24, was fired for allegedly neglecting his duties, and now he and Eva are on the run, Russian prosecutors say.

RUSSIA: *Had they both shot up? Sounds like it?* A doctor was arrested after he was called on to remove five grams of heroin from a drug mule's stomach – but then turned in only two grams. Police became suspicious when they arrived to collect the drugs and found both the suspect and the doctor high and unresponsive.

RUSSIA: A judge was caught napping while on the bench. He was fired after he sentenced a businessman to five years in prison for fraud – and the defendant's attorney posted videos showing the jurist sleeping on the bench. We learn that the defendant will get a new trial. *His name was Judge ZZZZZ...ZZZZ......*

POLAND

Poland has a civil law system. There is limited judicial review of legislative acts.

The country's highest court is Supreme Court or Sad Najwyzszy.

The chief of state is President Bronislaw Komorowski since August 6, 2010.

POLAND: *It was not alive!* It has been reported that a disturbed Warsaw woman has been taken into custody for allegedly trying to create a Frankencat. Police raided her home and found live cats and dogs and the corpses of hundreds of pets, many of which had been cut up and crudely recombined. The home was filled with stench. The woman told police she was trying to make an 'undead" feline.

Poland was overrun by both the German and the Soviet Union in World War II. It became a Soviet satellite following World War II, but its government was fairly tolerant and progressive. Labor turmoil in 1980 led to the formation of the independent trade union "Solidarity" movement which became a political force with over ten million members. Free elections in 1989 and 1990 brought the communist era to a close in Poland. Poland joined NATO in 1999 and the European Union in 2004.

POLAND: *He sounds like a real boob!* A man has sued his ex-wife for a refund, noting that he had spent $8,000 on her breast implants while they were married. Lukasz Molovik's lawyer said his client suffered "loss of use" of the 32 DD implants. Molovik didn't need legalese to explain his action. "To be frank about it," he said, "I didn't spend all that money so some other man can ogle her breasts instead of me."

POLAND: A man went under the knife for three hours to remove a screwdriver that had pierced his forehead. The 25-year-old man apparently lost consciousness after a fall. When he awoke he wasn't sure what had happened, so he went to his car, looked in the mirror and saw the screwdriver impaled just over his right eye. He had a cigarette, and then called a neighbor to help get him to the hospital. *YOOOOWWCCCCCCCCCHHHH!!*

CHAPTER FOUR

DUMBEST CRIMINALS FROM GERMANY, CENTRAL EUROPE AND SCANDANAVIA

Years ago, a much younger Professor Birdsong was stationed in Germany as a U.S. State Department officer. He had a great time living in Hamburg. He also had the opportunity to travel around Europe and Scandinavia. He has kept up with events in Germany ever since. Here are a few dumb criminal law stories from Germany, Central Europe and Scandinavia. Enjoy. *Ja voll!*

As Europe's largest economy and second most populous nation, after Russia, Germany is a key member of the continent's economic, political and defense organizations. European power struggles immersed Germany in two devastating World Wars in the first half of the 20th century and left the country occupied by the victorious Allied powers of the U.S., U.K., France and the Soviet Union in 1945. With the advent of the Cold War, two German states were formed in

1949; the western Federal Republic of Germany (FRG) and the eastern German Democratic Republic (GDR). The decline of the the USSR and the end of the Cold War allowed for German unification in 1990. Since then, Germany has expended considerable funds to bring eastern productivity and wages up to Western standards. In January 1999, Germany and ten other EU countries introduced a common European exchange currency, the euro.

Germany's legal system is a civil law system.

The country's highest court is the Federal Court of Justice.

The head of the government of Germany is Chancellor Angela Merkel.

GERMANY

GERMANY: *Bzzzzzz...* How awkward could this have been! A woman in Germany called police after hearing strange sounds coming from her bedroom, only to turn beet red when officers discovered that her vibrator had accidentally turned on in a drawer. "The tenant's face abruptly changed color," a police spokesman said. "The officers wished her a nice evening and left."

GERMANY: *There is a whole lot more to this story that we need to know...* The world's biggest underwear thief is now locked up. German police uncovered 1,000 pair of underpants after they caught a 46-year-old man swiping three more. He claimed he acquired them in car-trunk sales and over the Internet. *What does one do with 1,000 pair of underpants?*

GERMANY: *So What! Most U.S. Police cars have most of this same stuff in them!* German police say they stopped a driver who has wired his Ford Station wagon with an entire mobile office. Saarland police said late last year that the 35-year-old man was pulled over for doing 130 kph (80 mph) in a 100 kph zone while passing a truck. Built on a wooden frame on his passenger seat they found a laptop on a docking station tilted for easy driver access, a printer, router, wireless internet stick, WLAN antenna, and an inverter to power it all. A navigation system and cell phone mounted to the windshield completed the array. Since police had no evidence he used the office while driving, he got off with fine of what be about $153 speeding ticket and a possible fine for having unsecured items in his car.

GERMANY: *Too, too scary!! Stay out of the O.R.!* According to a German lawsuit, doctors left up to 16 surgical items in the body of a man in his 70's after a prostate cancer operation. When major complications arose, doctors went back in a removed needles, compresses and surgical strips. The victim died last year. We also learn from surveys that careless surgical teams in the U.S. leave items inside some 1,300 patients a year.

GERMANY: *"WIE SCHADE."(What a shame).* She wanted to be a working girl, but not *that* kind of working girl. A young woman got a shock when she went to an unemployment office looking for a job, and a clerk dispatched her to a brothel for an interview. It turned out the position involved serving customers refreshments and not herself. Nevertheless, the job listing did call for applicants to be "attractive" – raising a big socio-political ruckus across Germany.

GERMANY: *That must have been one long straightaway, wouldn't you say?* A truck driver lapsed into unconsciousness on a German highway – and the truck barreled six miles – before coming "by chance" to stop in a dirt bank outside a service station. No one was hurt as the truck headed along the road near Sinsheim and several times smacked into the central barrier while police diverted traffic. The driver was hospitalized with a heart problem. No charges were brought.

GERMANY: *Here's another one that sounds just like a plot stolen from the "Rise of the Planet of the Apes."* A group of chimpanzees managed to stage a jail break at a zoo in Germany after they fashioned pieces of wood from their enclosures into a makeshift ladder and climbed out. Four of the five escapees went back to their pen on their own. Zookeepers said the fifth was caught trying to "visit the head gorilla" at the zoo – perhaps to coordinate a simian uprising.

GERMANY: *This silly one will surely end in a plea to something lesser than attempted murder!* A 66-year-old man started trouble with his 63-year-old next door neighbor in a fight over a strip of lawn between their two properties. The older man poured a bucket of water over his neighbor's head for making too much noise while he was trimming the grassy strip. The soaked 63-year-old then attacked his older rival with a weed whacker. He was charged with attempted murder.

GERMANY: *Nope! It was not armed robbery. A man with no arms managed to steal* a TV from a German store. He made off with the 24-inch set using clamps that had been attached to his body by an accomplice. "It's hard to believe that the sight of an armless man walking along with a TV clamped to his body did not get anyone's attention," a police officer remarked. *Hands up! Ooopps...sorry....*

GERMANY: *A German crook decided to quit while he was still behind.* The 24-year-old tried to rob two hotels -- and in each case fled empty handed with security guards chasing him. Then he tried but failed to break into the local tax office in Muelheim an der Ruhr. Finally, the bandit wannabe gave up without a fuss after being trapped in a getaway van he used to ram an armored car. "He needs a change of job," said one police officer. *Sounds like he will get a new one in jail!*

GERMANY: *KA-BOOM!* A robbery gang in Malliss detonated a hugely powerful explosive device in an attempt to blast open a bank's ATM machine. The explosion practically destroyed the building -- but the ATM survived intact. It is further reported that the embarrassed thieves fled empty handed.

GERMANY: *What a bad investment!* German police billed a 19-year-old reptile lover $135,000 to pay for the massive emergency response required when his poisonous pet cobra escaped. It took three weeks of pulling up floorboards and evacuating apartments in the man's building before they found the slitherer -- who had died.

GERMANY: *Dude, it's cheaper to keep her...* A jealous husband in Germany hired assassins who four times botched hit jobs on his wife. The first attempt failed when the target never showed; the second when a group of school children disrupted the killer; a third came when a neighbor sauntered by; and finally when the woman managed to escape the attack.

GERMANY: *SIEG HEIL? (Hail Victory)* It is unlawful in Germany to manufacture, possess or display any objects glorifying the Third Reich. Recently, German prosecutors have been investigating an artist who created a series of garden gnomes with their arms raised in a Nazi salute. Investigators, however, are not sure if the artist is pro-Hitler or just ridiculing the Third Reich. "It will depend on what the artist and the owners of the gallery have to say for themselves," said a prosecution spokesman.

GERMANY: *Gesundhiet! (To your health)* It was reported in July 2009, that a car thief stole the limo of Germany's health minister while she was on vacation in Spain. Someone broke into the room of Health Minister Ulla Schmidt's chauffer, grabbed the car keys and made off with the black Mercedes, said a Health Ministry spokesperson.

GERMANY: *The King of the jungle rules!* A man who stole a van outside a German circus was so terrified when he realized there was a lion in the back that he crashed into a wall. The thief apparently noticed what his cargo was only when the big cat let out a bone-chilling roar. The cat was fine. The thief got away. No arrest was made.

GERMANY: *GOTT IN HIMMEL!!!* A German family returning home from a vacation trip departed their flight and discovered that their car was being used as an airport shuttle vehicle. They had left the car with a valet service. The surprised family members found the car – with a magnetic sign on the door bearing the name of the shuttle company – at a curb picking up passengers.

GERMANY: *Can you hear me now? Hello...Hello...* Police in Coburg recently pulled over a suspected drunken driver. They asked him to blow into a Breathalyzer, but the man thought it was a cell phone and tried to use it to call his lawyer. "We didn't really need the reading," one officer contended. "There aren't many sober people who would do that."

GERMANY: *What a way to go.* A lawyer's well-endowed lover allegedly tried to kill him with her breasts. German attorney Tim Schmidt's jealous girlfriend tried to smother him with her size 38DD bosoms because she said she wanted to make his death "as pleasant as possible," authorities say. She's been charged with attempted murder.

GERMANY: *"Treenappers?* A sapling cloned from the tree that lifted Anne Frank's spirits while she hid from the Nazis in Amsterdam has been felled and stolen from outside a school in Frankfort bearing the name of the Jewish teenager. Spokesman Manfred Fuellhardt said the 8-foot tree was stolen over the weekend from the grounds of the Anne Frank School. *"Treenappers?"*

GERMANY: *Next time, just send flowers Dumkopf!* A German woman called police after hearing someone climbing up her balcony. Police found it was just her boyfriend bringing flowers and a bottle of wine, but they still arrested him on an outstanding warrant. "He was trying to be romantic, but it all went wrong," said a police spokesperson. *What an Idiot!*

GERMANY: Two men were arrested in Offenbach after police saw a van at a gas station and thought there was something suspicious – then discovered 10 Shetland ponies crammed into the rear of the vehicle.

The men told the officers that they didn't even know the ponies were there. *Huh?*

GERMANY: *Be careful what you steal.* Bandits in Germany hot-wired and stole a van, unaware it carried cargo headed for a crematorium they drove off with 12 bodies. Nitwits! Wonder what they did with the bodies?

SWITZERLAND

Switzerland's sovereignty and neutrality have long been honored by the major European powers, and the country was not involved in either of the two world wars. The political and economic integration of Europe over the past half century, as well as Switzerland's role in many UN an international organizations, has strengthened Switzerland's ties with its neighbors. However, the country did not officially become a member of the UN until 2002.

Switzerland employs a civil law system.

Switzerland highest court is the Federal Supreme Court which consists of 38 judges.

The chief of state and head of government is the President of the Swiss Confederation Didier Burkhalter since January 1, 2014.

SWITZERLAND

SWITZERLAND: *It appears if one plans to hijack a plane to Switzerland; the Swiss would appreciate you doing it during regular business hours.* Recently, when an Ethiopian Airlines flight bound for Italy was commandeered by its co-pilot at 4 a.m. and ended up in Swiss airspace, calls to the nation' air force went unanswered because they quite work at 5 p.m. French jets were called to escort the plane safely to the Geneva airport.

SWITZLERLAND: A Swiss man thought he had a wonderful deal when he received a coupon which allowed him to drive a rare Ferrari 360 Spider FI Challenge Stradale for just $40. However, his dream turned into a nightmare when he crashed after 15 minutes behind the wheel. He now has to pay $400,000 to replace the car because his insurance will not cover the accident. *D'OH!*

NORWAY

In 1397, Norway was absorbed into a union with Denmark that lasted more than four centuries. In 1814, Norwegians resisted the cession of their country to Sweden and adopted a new constitution. Sweden then invaded Norway but agreed to let Norway keep its constitution in return for accepting the union under a Swedish king. Norway remained neutral in World War I and proclaimed its neutrality in World War II. Discovery of oil and gas in adjacent waters in the late 1960's boosted Norway's economic fortunes.

Norway employs a mixed legal system of civil, common and customary law.

Norway's highest court is the Supreme Court or Hoyesterett which consists of a chief justice and 18 associate justices.

The chief of state is King Harald V since January 17, 1991.

NORWAY

NORWAY: *Bang!* A hunter while trying to bag a moose fired an errant shot that pierced the wall of a cabin and struck a man sitting on his toilet. The injured man was air lifted to an Oslo area hospital with non-life-threatening wounds, police report. The hunter was aiming at the moose and possibly did not see the cabin more than 100 yards beyond the moose.

NORWAY: *Was she a bleeding liberal?* We understand that a vampire would have loved this show and tell, but a kindergarten teacher got fired for it. She brought in a sample of her own blood, poured it on a plate and let the children touch it. When they asked her how to remove it, "she put her bloody finger into her mouth and the children followed suit," said another teacher.

SWEDEN

A military power during the 17th century, Sweden has not participated in any war for almost two centuries. An armed neutrality was preserved in both World Wars. Sweden's long-successful economic formula of a capitalist system intermixed with substantial welfare elements was challenged in the late 1990's by high unemployment and in 2000-02 and, again, in 2009 by the global economic downturns. Fiscal discipline over the past several years has allowed the country to weather economic vagaries. Sweden joined the EU in 1995, but the public rejected the introduction of the euro in a 2003 referendum.

Sweden has a civil law system influenced by Roman-Germanic law and customary law.

The country's highest court is he Supreme Court of Sweden.

The chief of state is King Carl Gustaf XVI since September 19, 1973.

SWEDEN

SWEDEN: *How ridiculous!* Authorities in Sweden are insisting that a hotel install smoke detectors, even though it is made completely of ice. The Icehotel in the small Arctic town of Jukkasjaervi is a hotel that is rebuilt from huge blocks of ice each winter. Now authorities say the hotel must conform to regular building codes by installing smoke detectors before they can be allowed to have an occupancy permit. *RIDICULOUS!!*

SWEDEN: *It's called probable cause!* A teenage girl was arrested for robbing $370 in cash from a hamburger restaurant in Halmstad, after she posed for a bathroom-mirror photo holding the knife she used in the robbery. Police found the image on her cell phone when they went to her home to investigate, and then made the arrest. *Sounds as if she wanted to go to jail.*

SWEDEN: *OMG!* A police officer was docked five days' pay after he recorded a hot sex tape, while in uniform, in a police headquarters dressing room. He then sent the tape to a police colleague he had never met. Authorities ruled that the officer sexually molested the colleague and "violated their sexual integrity" by sending the sexy footage, according to reports.

SWEDEN: A Swedish TV news report on the civil war in Syria suddenly turned X-rated when a television in the background of the set started showing a pornographic film while the anchor was speaking. Viewers could clearly see a nude woman having sex. "Put simply, it's crap that it happened," said the embarrassed manager of TV4. *XXX XXX XXX!*

SWEDEN: *Send that invoice straight to the police department!* A woman mistakenly taken by the police from her home to a psychiatric hospital ended up with a $60 bill for the error. It appears that one of her neighbors in the town of Kalmar had called an emergency-service number and expressed suicidal thoughts. After the mistake was found and she was sent home she still received an invoice for $60 for the hospital visit.

SWEDEN: *Can we say that she busted the case wide open?* A woman has won a court fight to give her breast a proper burial. The woman from Jonkoping, had lost her breast after a surgical procedure, but didn't want it tossed out in a biological waste bank. Upon appealing to medical officials, they said there was no rule against keeping the amputated bosom and putting it to rest.

SWEDEN: *If at first you don't succeed, try and try again...* A murder suspect tried turning himself into police, only to be turned away because it was after hours and the Malmo police station was closed. "Closed? I'm suspected of murder and a wanted man. You guys really want to get a hold of me," the shocked suspect said into the intercom. The man, who allegedly killed a gang leader two years ago, gave up for the night, and then turned himself in the next day.

SWEDEN: We wonder what her husband had done to her? A woman admitted stabbing her husband to death with a fillet knife she had received as a Christmas present from her employers. Swedish police said that after the attack on her husband, Jeanette Javell, 42, wrote a bizarre note to her boss stating, "Thank you for the Christmas gift...By the way it worked!" *OMG, that's cold!*

SWEDEN: A 27-year-old man was exonerated of drug charges after he told authorities he unknowingly ate a cake laced with THC, the chemical found in marijuana. A court in Ostersund cleared the man after finding he had accidently eaten the substance. He had been arrested during a traffic stop on his way home from a dinner party. *Justice prevails...*

HOLLAND

After a 20-year French occupation, a Kingdom of the Netherlands was formed in 1815. In 1830 Belgium seceded and formed a separate kingdom. The Netherlands remained neutral in World War I and suffered invasion by Germany in World War II. A modern industrialized nation, the Netherlands is also a large exporter of agricultural products. The country was a founding member of NATO and of the EU and participated in the introduction of the euro in 1999.

The Netherlands legal system is a civil law system based on the French system.

The country's highest court is the Supreme Court or the Hoge Raad.

The chief of state is King Willem-Alexander since April 30, 2013.

HOLLAND

HOLLAND: *I bet they always had men coming and going – and both too soon!* We learn that twin sisters who may be the oldest professionals in the world's oldest profession have retired after 50 years. Louise and Martines Fokkens, 70, say they serviced some 355,000 customers in their careers as legal brothel babes in Amsterdam. They claim they hung up their fishnet stockings due to arthritis.

HOLLAND: *Those must have been some huge shipping crates!* Authorities seized a mountain of cocaine hidden in boxes of fruit that were being shipped to the Rotterdam Zoo. Dutch prosecutors maintain that more than eight tons of cocaine was hidden among the bananas aboard a ship from Ecuador.

ICELAND

Settled by Norwegian and Celtic (Scottish and Irish) immigrants during the late 9th and 10th centuries A.D. Iceland boasts the world's oldest functioning legislative assembly, the Althing, established in 930. Independent for over 300 years, Iceland was subsequently ruled by Norway and Denmark. Fallout from a large volcano eruption in 1875 devastated the Icelandic economy and caused widespread famine. Over the next 25 years, 20 percent of the island's population emigrated, mostly to Canada and the U.S. The second half of the 20th century saw substantial economic growth driven primarily by the fishing industry. The economy diversified greatly after the country joined the European Economic Area in 1994, but Iceland was especially hard hit by the global financial crisis following 2008.

Iceland's legal system is a civil law system influenced by the Danish model.

Iceland's highest Court is the Supreme Court of Haestirettur which consists of 9 judges.

The chief of state is President Olafur Ragnar Grimsson since August 1, 1996.

ICELAND

ICELAND: *Sounds like peace loving country.* Police in Iceland had never fatally shot a criminal until early December of 2013. Officers in Reykjavik gunned down a man who fired on a SWAT team with a shotgun. The national police chief said the incident was "without precedent."

Undoubtedly!

CHAPTER FIVE

DUMBEST CRIMINAS FROM THE UNITED KINGDOM AND FRANCE

The first half of the 20th century saw the United Kingdom's strength seriously depleted in two

world wars and the Irish Republic's withdrawal from the union. The second half witnessed the dismantling of the Empire and the UK rebuilding itself into a modern and prosperous European nation. As one of five permanent members of the UN Security Council and a founding member of NATO and the Commonwealth, the UK pursues a global approach to foreign policy. The UK is also an active member of the EU, although it chose to remain outside of the Economic and Monetary Union.

The British legal system is a common law system.

The highest court is the Supreme Court which consists of 12 justices, including the court president and the deputy president.

The chief of state is Her Majesty Queen Elizabeth II since February 6, 1952.

Professor Birdsong has had the opportunity to visit France and the United Kingdom on several occasions. He finds that France is lovely. He is not so much in love with England because of the strange language they speak there that they call English. They also have lots of dumb criminal law stories. Here are a few...

ENGLAND:

ENGLAND: *Those bad old doctors need a big bust in the mouth*! A 23-year- old British woman convinced her doctors that she needed taxpayer-funded breast-enhancement surgery to boost her flagging mental health. Now the Leeds woman is unhappy with having gone from a 32A to a 36DD – and wants to sue the doctors for making her breasts too big. "I was rushed through the process. I didn't actually ask for 36DD. I would have been happier with a B cup," said the woman.

ENGLAND: *We wonder whether Viagra had anything to do with this*. A 59-year-old British man believed he had a lot to crow about in the bedroom! As a matter of fact, he called emergency police services 30 times during a four hour period to brag about his sexual prowess with women in his bedroom. Police authorities were not very impressed. They traced his calls, went to his home that same night and arrested him for wasting police resources.

ENGLAND: *About time!* We've learned recently that British spies who are chasing suspects finally have permission to exceed the posted speed limits. Members of MI5 and MI6 intelligence services will no longer have to worry about receiving tickets as long as they can prove they were on a covert operation or surveillance.

ENGLAND: *What the frack?* A pair of anti-fracking protesters in England thought they might strike a blow for their cause by gluing themselves to a gas pump at a station owned by a company involved in the fracking process. Unfortunately, they did not realize that the station had been sold. The new owner, who never "fracked" in his life, contended he was "very annoyed" with the glued protestors.

ENGLAND: Around Valentine's Day earlier this years a London shop offered scorned lovers specialty made voodoo dolls of their former flames. Customers could mail in photos of their exes a get a choice of five hexes.

Hey, who do that voodoo like they dooo???

ENGLAND: *KA-BOOM!* Zeus, a 6-month-old British part greyhound mutt, blew up his master's house by chewing through a deodorant can. The can leaked flammable fumes near a hot water heater, which exploded when the back burner came on. It is reported that no one was hurt. The owner, Barry Bane said, "He's just a pup and at the moment he'll chew through anything."

ENGLAND: *A scam artist betrayed by his own tattoos?* Kent Andrews and his baby-mama Vicky T were able to scam $80,000 from British social services when he pretended to be her landlord in order to collect rent checks from the government. The scam went smoothly over a number of years until a social worker finally noticed that the purported "landlord" was actually tattooed with the names of her children.

ENGLAND: *Oh my!* This reported burglary led police to an investigation in the attempted theft of Sigmund Freud's ashes. Police in London reported that thieves tried to take an urn from a crematorium that held Freud's remains. The police officers were not afraid to express how they felt about the attempted crime, decrying the "despicable act" that "defies belief." *This sounds oh so British!*

ENGLAND: *She must have not been much of a girlfriend*. A British man was arrested for having sex with his girlfriend's dog after she discovered a cellphone video of him fornicating with the pup. The 19-year-old admitted to having sex with the bull terrier after his girlfriend took his phone to the police and showed them the footage. Police also found marijuana in his possession when he was placed under arrest. *What a pot headed creep!*

ENGLAND: A shopkeeper in Ramsbottom fought off a robbery attempt with the only weapon at his disposal – beer. When a masked bandit waved a gun and demanded money at the Bargain Booze store, the astute worker grabbed cans of lager from behind the counter and threw them at the assailant's head. The flurry of cans drove the robber away empty handed.

ENGLAND: A library book overdue by 63 years was returned to the library in Warwickshire, after amnesty was offered. The fine for the return of the 1950 edition of *Pinocchio* was capped at $8.35, when it could have drawn an overdue fine of $6,600.

ENGLAND: A bomb at a British pub turned out not to be a blow up device. When a person spotted a silver suitcase left behind in the Gardeners Arms in Brentwood, the place was evacuated and the local police bomb squad investigated. What did they find? They found the case contained a hair dryer. *Nothing to see here – go home. It's only a hair dryer!*

ENGLAND: *Ha, Ha...* A British man put his girlfriend up for sale on eBay. Although he described the girlfriend, Moira Deborah, as an "old woman" who couldn't do house work, Shaun C received dozens of bids, topping off at $1,181. He later admitted it was all a joke. *Ha, Ha...*

ENGLAND: Officials in London hounded a woman to pay a parking ticket – even though it was for $0. JW, 40, was shocked when she found the ticket reading "0.00 Pounds" on her windshield, and she ignored it. After much red tape JW eventually straightened out the mistake.

ENGLAND: *Flatulence city, maybe?* A thief stole 6,000 cans of baked beans from a food delivery truck in England. The bandit struck when the driver fell asleep and he is still at large. Beans, beans, good for the heart, the more you eat the more you...

ENGLAND: *THUD!* A Gambian man awaiting deportation in a British detention center was so upset that he wasn't allowed to see his home country's soccer team play on television, he ran head first into a wall and became paralyzed. We learn that Amadou Nyang is now suing the British government for not stopping him from expressing his team loyalty.

ENGLAND: *The headline read: "Being an incorrigible rogue is no longer illegal."* The British Ministry of Justice reported that the offense, created in the early 19th century, was one of more than 300 obsolete offenses which have been abolished over the past year. The legislative history reveals that the 1824 Vagrancy Act was passed to deter and punish "idle and disorderly persons." The law defined an "incorrigible rogue" as a homeless person who resisted arrest or escaped confinement. *Just so British!*

ENGLAND: *Was the drive-by done by the Crips or the Bloods?* A 40-year-old man in England was seriously injured in a drive-by slingshot attack. Police report the victim was hit in the eye when someone fired the slingshot from inside a passing car.

ENGLAND: *Quick, give that guy some "stress balls" to squeeze...* A British man's job was to pack "stress balls" – but he became really stressed when he was fired. The 44-year-old warehouse worker from Blackpool allegedly punched the manager who discharged him from his temporary job with the company that sells novelty products. A prosecutor said other staffers arrived and the accused man pulled out knives and shouted, "I'll cut you up." *Temper, temper!*

ENGLAND: *The police could clearly see he's nuts!* An Englishman was arrested after he was found strolling around Plymouth in nothing but a blonde wig, pink gloves and pink shoes. Malcolm King, 55, also allegedly had a bottle of vodka and his face was covered with hair removal cream.

ENGLAND: *What's the big deal? Last time I was in England, Queen Elizabeth's picture was already on many bank notes?* We learn a London man has been arrested and charged with tweeting threats against the feminist who led a successful social-media campaign to get a woman's face on a British bank note. Caroline Criado-Perez said she had faced a deluge of Twitter abuse – including threats to rape and kill her – since the Bank of England announced recently that Jane Austen's picture will appear on the new 10 pound notes.

ENGLAND: *Cruel and heartless grave keepers?* A grieving woman was fined for leaving too many flowers on her daughter's grave. Emma Townsend was slapped with a $133 ticket for placing more than one bouquet at the grave at a government-run cemetery in Derbyshire. Townsend found the summons attached to her daughter's gravestone.

ENGLAND: *Obviously, neither of the suspects could play the dang thing!* British police recently recovered a $1.8 million antique violin stolen from an acclaimed musician in 2010. South Korean violinist Min-Jin Kym was eating at a London sandwich shop in November of 2010 when she noticed her case containing the 300 year old Stradivarius was missing. The police recovered the violin intact with minor damage. Two suspects have been jailed and charged with the theft. The violin was made in 1696, and is one of only 400 in the entire world.

ENGLAND: *A blockheaded namesake!* We learn that British Bobbies arrested Ronald McDonald for entering a McDonald's restaurant. Violating a restraining order, a man who shares his name with the fast food chain, followed his estranged wife into a McDonald's in Kent demanding to speak to her. It is further reported that he was not "fried" but he did receive a three month jail stay.

ENGLAND: *The kid's got chutzpa.* An 11-year-old British boy did not have a ticket, but that did not stop him. The youngster managed to sneak past security at Manchester Airport and board an Italy bound jet, even though he lacked a passport, a boarding pass and a guardian. Liam Corcoran was discovered shortly before the Jet2.com plane landed in Rome. He was soon put on another plane back home.

ENGLAND: *What a bizarre delusion...Insanity will do that to one*! A British driver had a close encounter of the 5-0 kind. The crazed man rammed his car into a police vehicle while speeding because he believed he was being chased by space aliens. Brett Webber continued driving and was finally caught when police popped his tires. He was found chanting, "Doh, ray, me, soh," because he thought it would ward off the outer space visitors. Fortunately, no one was hurt.

ENGLAND: *Probably reaching for more booze, no doubt!* A Briton in West Sussex looked into his 35-year-old friend's kitchen window, saw him reaching into a cupboard and greeted him. The fellow did not respond, or move. Turns out that he had died, and the body had apparently gotten snagged on a cabinet. The coroner said the man had been crazy drunk in his home, banged his head and died while reaching for something.

ENGLAND: *...But thinner is supposed to be better!* How about this for getting out of paying traffic tickets? British drivers in Coventry could be getting quite a break as lawyers fight to overturn six years' worth of traffic tickets – because the government used the wrong font on speed limit signs. The offending font has taller and thinner numbers.

ENGLAND: *Sounds like too much freaky-deeky sexy-wexy going on*! Kinky sex in England has gotten more risqué since the publication of the book "Fifty Shades of Grey." It has gotten so risqué that it is now affecting local fire departments. Officials in London say that fire brigades in the country are being called out constantly to help people who get stuck in handcuffs.

ENGLAND: *HIC!* A drunken woman shouted "I'm Jack Sparrow" (Johnny Depp's character in "Pirates of the Caribbean") at police as she floated off in a 50 foot ferryboat she had stolen by cutting its dock rope lines. It is reported that she was soon captured and thrown in the brig to sleep it off.

ENGLAND: Six Brits allegedly took part in a convenience store robbery in the town of Whitnash, and then ran off to an apartment complex. Incredulous police tracked down the suspects by following their footprints in the snow. *D'OH! What idiots...*

ENGLAND: *Naked and crazy, too. We wonder whether he did this year round.* England gets mighty cold in winter...A Brit's naked ambition to be a champion of nudity has landed him in jail again. Stephen Gough, 54, defied a judge's order to wear enough clothes to at least cover his private parts – and was taken to jail wearing only his boots, socks and a knapsack. Gough, who believes unfettered nudity is a human right, has walked naked all over England and has spent a lot of time behind bars and before judges.

ENGLAND: *GAG!* British customs agents seized 207 pounds of dead caterpillars from the luggage of a 22 year old passenger last month. The traveler told agents at Gatwick Airport near London that the caterpillars were intended for personal consumption.

ENGLAND: *Tally-Ho!* A McDonald restaurant refused to serve a woman trying to go through the drive-thru atop a horse. So the horsewoman angrily took the horse inside the restaurant and tried to order at the counter. A report about the incident revealed that the police were called after the animal left a "tip" on the floor.

ENGLAND: *Idiot!* An accused burglar fleeing police in Camberwell jumped into a tall garbage bin in a park where officers found him upside down. Cleese Buck, 22, told arresting officers he had been playing goal in a soccer match, which would account for the gloves he was wearing, but he had no explanation for his garbage bin hiding place.

SCOTLAND

SCOTLAND: *He should have gone to Italy for good pizza, not Scotland.* A German tourist got into a raging fight with his wife in a Scottish pizza parlor over how bad their vacation was going and threw a sizzling hot pizza at her. Wolfgang Gruelich, 57, was let out of jail after he agreed to take a separate flight home from his family.

SCOTLAND: Prison officials in Scotland transferred a pre-operative transsexual man who was serving 18 years for a torture slaying. Why did they transfer him? He was transferred from a woman's prison after he was caught having sex with some of the women. It appears that prison officials were a bit premature by putting him in with the women.

SCOTLAND: *We're certain this addiction is easier to beat than a cocaine addiction.* A man in Scotland was hospitalized in critical condition after overdosing on Brussels sprouts, which facilitate blood clotting. Like spinach and kale, Brussels sprouts contain large amounts of vitamin K, which thickens blood.

SCOTLAND: Here is a story that may recount the first time anyone was actually held responsible for trying to get a dummy elected to public office. A lady in Aberdeen was arrested on charges that she illegally entered into a town council election a mannequin under the name "Helena Torry." The lady, who on a nominating petition wrote the dummy a fabricated biography, is fighting the charges. Of course, the mannequin will lose the election because of all the dummies already in elected office!!

WALES

WALES: *This is so bogus; this town must be really hard up for revenue!* A Welch woman has been hit with a fine of more than $600 – for dropping a single packet of salt in a KFC parking lot. The woman was eating some fried chicken in the lot when a town official saw her drop the small packet of salt. When she could not produce $118 on the spot for this littering violation, she was ordered to go to court and pay some $500 more.

FRANCE

France today is one of the most modern countries in the world and is a leader among European nations. It plays an influential global role as a permanent member of the United Nations Security Council, NATO, the G-8, the G-20 and the EU. In recent decades, its reconciliation and cooperation with Germany have proved central to the economic integration of Europe, including the introduction of a common currency, the euro. In the early 21st century, five French overseas entities – French Guyana, Guadeloupe, Martinique, Mayotte, and Reunion – became French regions and were made part of France proper.

The French legal system is a civil law system.

The highest court is the Court of Cassation or Cour de Cassation.

The head of state is President Francois Hollande since May 15, 2012.

FRANCE: *Sacre Bleu!* Police in Marseille have arrested 24-year-old twin brothers after one of them was matched by DNA to a series of rapes. Yet, police can't figure out which one did it – because normal genetic tests can't differentiate between identical twins.

FRANCE: *This is one sad and lonely story.....* 15 years and no one missed him. The body of a man was discovered in his bed in a home in the city of Lille – 15 years after he died. Police say the house had been thought to be abandoned and nobody had missed the occupant.

FRANCE: *More crazies on the loose, we should be very afraid...* In July 2013 Interpol, which is based in France, issued a global alert for hundreds of al Qaeda terrorists, many of them sentenced to death, who escaped in a mass jail break near Baghdad during that month. It is reported that at least 140 senior al Qaeda commanders were among 1,035 prisoners freed during planned attacks on the Abu Ghraib and Taji prisons, by a group known as the Islamic State in Iraq and Greater Syria which is an al Qaeda affiliate.

FRANCE: *Trifecta of mayhem?* A soldier in the northern city of Caen maimed three of his fellow soldiers after his live "souvenir" anti-tank rocket fell from his wall. The weapon exploded, and one soldier lost his legs, the second lost a testicle and the third lost his hearing.

FRANCE: *Oh mummy, how we missed you!* A story from Paris maintained that an apartment for sale there had everything: vaulted ceilings, marble counter tops, and a mummified body. A man who bought the apartment at auction arrived with the door keys and found the hanged corpse of the previous resident. The building manager had apparently never looked inside the apartment after the resident had disappeared.

CHAPTER SIX

DUMBEST CRIMINALS FROM OUR HEMISPHERE: CANADA, MEXICO, AND BRAZIL

Canada is our beloved neighbor to the north. Professor Birdsong presents you here with several dumbest criminals law stories from our northern neighbor.

A land of vast distances and rich natural resources, Canada became a self-governing dominion in 1867 while retaining ties to the British crown. Economically and technologically, the nation has developed in parallel with the U.S., its neighbor to the south across the world's longest unfortified border. Canada faces the political challenges of meeting public demand for quality improvements in health care, education, social service, and economic competitiveness, as well as responding to the particular concerns of predominantly francophone Quebec.

Canada's legal system is a common law system except in Quebec where civil law is based on the French civil code.

The highest court is the Supreme Court of Canada.

The head of state is her Majesty Queen Elizabeth II since February 6, 1952.

CANADA

CANADA: A drug-treatment center in Vancouver has installed a crack-pipe vending machine at its facility – going retail in an effort to reach hard-core addicts and keep them from spreading diseases by sharing pipes. It is reported that the bright, polka-dotted machine dispenses crack pipes like candy, only cheaper: Each glass pipe cost a quarter. Defenders say coin-op crack pipes are a better deal for addicts, who risk catching HIV and hepatitis C by sharing and reusing damaged, disease-spreading pipes bought off the street at much higher prices. It has been reported that the Portland hotel Society which runs Vancouver's legally sanctioned injection site and treatment center installed the vending machine six months earlier.

CANADA: *He was in the right place at the right time.* A Saskatoon resident was depressed as he rode a cab to work after his car was stolen – until he spotted someone driving the stolen vehicle. The victim immediately demanded the cabby "to follow that car" and was able to catch up to the alleged thieves, who fled on foot but were soon arrested.

CANADA: Earlier this year a Calgary resident made a great real estate offer. He offered to give his home away to anyone who could come and truck it away. Hastie Jasper said he wanted to build a new home on his lot, and anyone who wanted his 1,200-square-foot bungalow can cart it away. We have no information whether there were any takers.

CANADA: The annual Iceman marathon in northern British Columbia, in which competitors test themselves against the coldest of temperatures on skis, skates and foot had to be cancelled this past winter. Why? It was too cold! The organizers maintained that they needed temperatures of a least minus-20 degrees. However, when the thermometers would not rise above minus-28, they had to call off the endurance test on health related grounds.

CANADA: *Who the heck buys all those cookies?* Police investigating an attempted home-invasion- robbery uncovered an apparent marijuana ring that dabbled in baking. A 22-year-old man in Surrey, east of Vancouver, BC, told police he fought two would be robbers who beat him with a crowbar – but police detectives discovered that the alleged victim was part of a marijuana operation that had churned out 8,000 pot-laced cookies.

CANADA: *Decency demands that the dolls be fully clothed!* Wicked Wanda's Adult Emporium in Ottawa has created a Christmas window display showing Barbie and Ken dolls engaged in a variety of sex acts inspired by the best-selling erotic novel "Seven Shades of Grey." Some of the dolls wear leather and chains, while others wield whips. A number of city residents have complained to authorities about the sex scenes. However, Wanda contends that the S & M scenes are not unlawful because all of the dolls are fully clothed. So silly...

CANADA: *The headline read: "The medium was the message."* A Montreal artist used dog poop to paint a portrait of Superior Court Judge Claudine Ray, because she dismissed a lawsuit he filed. When police advised him to see a psychiatrist, he complained they were trying to censor him.

CANADA: *Government regulation run wild?* A letter carrier refused to deliver mail to a home in Winnipeg because one of the front steps was two inches higher than the 12 inch step requirement limit that the Canadian post office puts on private homes. The homeowner is appealing the decision, but he may have to use more email.

CANADA: *She's no boob!* A woman, allegedly shot, by her ex-boyfriend says she was saved by her breast implants. She testified in a Toronto court that the bullets went through both implants before inflicting a minor arm wound. She was so pleased with her bulletproof chest, she got two new implants.

CANADA: Oh poot! Police in Ontario have announced the winner of their silliest excuse competition. She is a woman stopped for speeding who explained that she stepped on the accelerator when she adjusted her seating position to fart.

CANADA: *BANG, BANG....* Lady Gaga fired up controversy and drew fierce criticism from gun control advocates at her January show in Vancouver where she had donned a skimpy top outfitted with plastic assault rifles covering her breasts. It was not the first time one of Gaga's garments packed such firepower. She wore bra outfitted with two automatic weapons on a July 20120 cover for Rolling Stone magazine.

CANADA: *Johnson probably didn't report her missing right away because he was happy that she had left!* Police are trying to clear the name of a man suspected of killing his wife back in the 1960's when she disappeared. Marvin Johnson, who died in the 1990's, became a suspect because he didn't report his wife, Lucy, missing until she had been gone for four years. Police in a Vancouver suburb highlighted the cold case recently and discovered that Lucy had simply left and remarried and was living under a different name in a different town.

CANADA: *OMG, How insensitive to rhinos, too!* A Canadian beer was taken off menus – because it violated human rights. A craft brew called "Albino Rhino" was banned after a woman with albinism filed a complaint with the British Columbia human rights Tribunal claiming the name was insensitive to people with her condition. The beer will be renamed "Rhino" which the BC Animal rights Tribunal will probably be hearing about soon.

CANADA: *Rogue bottlers... Oh, Puleeeze...* A gang of sticky-fingered bandits stole $30 million of maple syrup from a warehouse in Quebec, where the syrup was stored in huge barrels. The amount stolen was so vast that traders on the Canadian commodities market fear the syrup could be sold to rogue bottlers, causing a crash in wholesale prices and an upheaval on store shelves.

CANADA: *What a good hearted jerk!* A family in Guelph, Ontario that had not realized their home had been burglarized were surprised get to all their stolen possessions back the next day with an apology. When the family arrived back home after a short trip they hadn't noticed a screen door had been cut and an Xbox and a digital camera were missing. The next morning they found a plastic bag hanging on the front door containing the electronics, $450 to fix the door and an anonymous note stating, "I have been having a very hard time financially lately and I made the worst mistake of my life."

CANADA: *Oh Fukme!* A Montreal judge has ordered a sushi shop to stop calling itself Fukyu. The judge conceded that it might be an innocent Japanese word for a form of martial arts – but ruled that "it was clearly inappropriate" in Canada. Restaurant owner John De Melo, who apparently believes any publicity is good publicity, wasn't upset at the ruling. He claimed that the case made potential diners aware of his restaurant.

CANADA: *Who knew! No arms, no real violation. Impossibility at common law!* Police in Saskatoon, Saskatchewan, ticketed a driver for not wearing his seatbelt. The driver, Steve Simonar, is vowing to fight the ticket – because he has no arms and can't buckle up. Simonar, who lost his arms up to the shoulders in a 1985 power line accident, drives using a left-foot steering wheel in a government-approved vehicle.

CANADA: *If that's the law, then the law is an ass!* A police officer has been charged with failing to investigate a hate crime against him. Constable Dameian Muirhead, who is black, was threatened with lynching by a gang of drunken thugs when he went to break up a wild party on a farm outside Toronto. Because Muirhead decided to ignore the threat, he is now in trouble with his police department and facing a disciplinary hearing.

CANADA: *Silly, silly neighbors...Shame on them. Thanks Baton Rouge!* A 9-year-old boy turned a lemon into lemonade. Neighbors complained that Corbin potter was selling lemonade without a permit on their block – to raise money for a children's hospital. The police shut the kid down. However, owners of Baton Rouge, a restaurant in Whitby, Ontario, say they will let Corbin put up his lemonade stand in front of their restaurant in August, with all the proceeds of sales going to Toronto's Hospital for Sick Children.

MEXICO

The site of several advanced Amerindian civilizations – including the Olmec, Toltec, Maya and Aztec – Mexico was conquered and colonized by Spain in the early 16th century and was administered by Spain for nearly three centuries. It achieved its independence early in the 19th century. The global financial crisis beginning in late 2008 caused a massive economic downturn the following year, although growth returned quickly in 2010. Ongoing economic and social concerns in Mexico include low real wages, underemployment for large segments of the population, inequitable income distribution, and drug trafficking organizations that have led to bloody feuding resulting in tens of thousands of drug related homicides in the last fifteen years.

The legal system is a civil law system with U.S constitutional law influence

The highest court is the Supreme Court of Justice or Suprema Corte de Justicia de la Nacion.

The chief of state and head of the government is President Enrique Pena Nieto.

MEXICO: *Drats!* Mexico City prison officials foiled an inmate's scheme to have his dead mother smuggle in a cell phone. Inmates at Santa Maria Acatitla Prison can have the casket of a parent or child brought to the prison yard for a final farewell. However, guards found an illegal cell phone hidden the casket of the mother and confiscated it. *Drats!*

MEXICO: *Ninny – this is no way to use a skateboard!* A would be bank robber rode up to a bank in Mexico City on a skateboard and announced a robbery. He may have made a strange getaway on his skateboard, but the teller set off a silent alarm and the robber waited while she counted out the money. Police then showed up and arrested the man.

MEXICO: *A few more prostitutes and they can hold their first "ho down."* A group in Mexico has convinced the government to create the first retirement home for elderly street walkers. The home in Tepito, called Casa Xochiquetzal, can house up to 45 retired prostitutes, and now has 23.

MEXICO: *RIGHT!* Members of the "Knights Templars," a Mexican drug gang has just issued a "code of conduct" handbook to each of its members.　　The code mandates that gang members shall treat women and children well, not kill only for money and refrain from drug use. It also suggests regular drug testing for members.

BRAZIL

Following more than three centuries under Portuguese rule, Brazil gained its independence in 1822, maintaining a monarchical system of government until the abolition of slavery in 1888 and the subsequent proclamation by the military in 1889. By far the largest and most populous country in South America in the 20th century, Brazil underwent more than a half century of populist and military government until 1985, when the military regime peacefully ceded power to civilian rule. Today Brazil is South America's leading economic power and regional leader, one of the first in the area to begin an economic recovery. The country is beset by high income inequality and crime problems. The country will host the summer Olympics in 2016.

The legal system is a civil law system – a new civil code was enacted in 2002, replacing the 1916 code.

The highest court is Supreme Federal Court

The chief of state and the head of government is President Dilma Rousseff since January 1, 2011

BRAZIL

BRAZIL: *Ay, Mamacita!!!!!!* A woman has been charged with attempted murder for putting a toxic chemical on her private parts in an effort to poison her husband during love-making. The man wound up in the hospital after the noxious roll in the hay, but he survived. The woman was caught when a test turned up the foul substance.

BRAZIL: *Sounds like no Bzzzzzzzzzzzzz.....* A man held up a sex shop in Brasilia, walking out with a $4,000 gold plated vibrator. The clerk, noting the bandit forgot the charger, said, "I really don't know what he'll do with it. We'll leave it to his imagination."

BRAZIL: *Seems the residents wanted to "blow" the election!* A lady running for city council in the town of Itacoatiara drew the attention of police who noticed a "huge" crowd gathering around her car on Election Day. An officer searched the vehicle and found hundreds of her leaflets – with packages of cocaine attached. Residents said she had been giving them out in exchange for promises to vote for her.

BRAZIL: *"LET IT BE."* The city of Belo Horizonte has been hit by a crime wave – by crooks all named John Lennon. Three Beatles bandits were arrested in one month and a fourth Lennon criminal was found dead. A police official says the name John Lennon is common in Brazil since the singer's 1980 death in New York City.

CHAPTER SEVEN

DUMBEST CRIMINALS FROM A FEW OTHER COUNTRIES

Yes, these are the final few dumbest criminal law stories from a few other countries of our far flung planet – all in alphabetical order! Read 'em all for a few last laughs.

ARGENTINA: *Edith, you are a moron! You must have a death wish...* A 22-year-old woman wants to marry the man who was convicted of killing her twin sister. Edith Casas believes Victor Cingolani who was her sister's boyfriend, is innocent, and wants to marry him in prison. Her mother, however, has other ideas, and has gone to court to put a halt to the wedding plans.

AUSTRIA: *Weird stuff?* We learn that the world's first robot suicide has taken place in Austria. The Irobot Roomba 760 cleaned its owners' kitchen. In November 2013, when the robot finished its kitchen chores the owners turned it off for the night. The robot restarted itself, climbed on the stove, pushed a pot out of the way and turned on the burners. We learn, further, that no suicide note was found.

GREECE: *YUCK*...A court has ruled that this jail break was justified! The court in the port city of Igoumenitsa acquitted 15 allegedly illegal immigrants who broke out of a small, filthy jail with no running water, no bedding and one chemical toilet. The men escaped by pushing past police guard who entered the cell to clean out garbage

IRAQ: *He who lives by the sword dies by the...* In February 2014, an instructor teaching his militant recruits how to make car bombs accidently set off explosives in his demonstration, killing 21 of them in a huge blast that alerted authorities to the existence of the rural training camp in an orchard north of Baghdad. Nearly two dozen people were arrested, including wounded insurgents trying to hobble away from the scene. The militants belonged to the network now known as the Islamic State of Iraq and Syria, an extremist group that broke away from al Qaeda.

ISRAEL: A Palestinian prisoner somehow got his sperm smuggled out to his wife. Abdul Kareem al-Rimawi, in jail for attacking an Israeli soldier, got the sperm out to his wife and they had a baby. We just do not believe this story! Sperm only survives for 72 hour under the best of conditions....*We think his wife has been canoodling with someone else!*

ITALY: *Merry Dildo?* An outdoor Christmas tree in Milan had to be cleaned up after city officials removed dildos and other sex toys that had been placed on the tree as ornaments. A Milanese woman who has launched an Italian sex toy e-commerce website defended the "Tree of Pleasure," which she said was intended to end taboos by making the items "normal everyday objects."

ITALY: *OINK!* It has been reported that a still-breathing Italian mob boss was fed to the pigs by members of a rival crime syndicate. Francesco Raccosta was beaten with iron bars by members of the N'drangheta crime family which controls much of the southern Italian region of Calabria. They then tossed him in the pig sty where he was eaten alive. The murder was allegedly carried out by mob boss Simone Pepe, 24, who admitting to the killing and three other murders. Raccosta had been missing for more than a year when authorities arrested Pepe and gained his confession. A police spokesman said the bloody feuds between the rival crime clans had been ongoing since the 1950's.

ITALY: Italian police have turned to twitter to crack down on Rome's creative parking scofflaws who routinely leave their motor scooters and cars on sidewalks in the middle of busy streets. Citizens who see illegally parked cars can now alert a police Twitter account, @PLRomaCapitale. Police vow to rush to the scene and ticket or tow the offending vehicles. *Right! My experience reveals that Italian police never "rush" any place.*

ITALY/GERMANY: *It appears that we have a young punk in the making, folks!* A 13-year-old boy ran away in style – when he left Italy in his adoptive father's Mercedes Benz and actually made it 500 miles in an attempt to see his birth family in Poland. The boy, said to be a good go-cart driver, drove the automatic for nearly a day before German police stopped him near Leipzig. He set off after arguing with his adopted mother.

KENYA: *Baaaaa! Baaaaa!* A rapist was convicted in Kenya after testimony from the victim – a goat. Katana Kitsao Gona was forced to be confronted by his accuser in a courtroom when officials brought in the goat at his bestiality trial and the goat, reportedly, started bleating repeatedly. Gona, who had been found naked with the animal in a farmer's field, was found guilty and given a ten year prison sentence.

KENYA: A soccer referee has filed a lawsuit contending that he's been left impotent ever since a coach ran onto the field to protest a call – and grabbed his testicles. Referee Martin Wekesa is suing the national soccer federation, seeking $240,000 in compensation. Wekesa said that after he ejected a player from a game last year, he was attacked by Soarki Youth team players and then by Daudi Kajembe, a member of the coaching staff. Wekesa said the coach "attacked me in my private parts. I was crying and could not get myself out from his hands. *OOOOOOOOOOUUUUUUUUCCCCCHHHHH!*

NIGERIA: A new law signed by the president of Nigeria in January 2014, without announcement, has made it illegal for gay people to even hold a meeting. The "Same Sex

Marriage Prohibition Act" also criminalizes homosexual clubs, associations and organizations, with penalties of up to 14 years in prison. We learn the act has drawn condemnation from the United States and Britain. It is reported that some gays have already fled the country.

SAUDI ARABIA: *Nothing like getting rid of the competition!* Three men were recently deported from the country because they were declared "too handsome" for the Muslim country. The men were visiting from the United Arab Emirates when they were spotted by Saudi religious officials at a cultural festival. The Saudis arrested the men and told them that they were so handsome that they might tempt local women to fall in love with them. They were deported back to the UAE.

SERBIA: *These are very weird people. She's dead, chasing other women sounds saner...* How was this for a dying last wish? When Milena Markovic of Belgrade was dying she asked her husband, Milan, to have a replica of her vagina engraved on her tombstone, so he would look at it instead of "chasing other women." We learn it took Milan nearly three years to find a stonecutter up to the task. "Now that it is finished, I love it," said Milan.

SPAIN: *What do terrorists smell like?* Authorities may soon have a new way to sniff out terrorists. Scientists in Spain are working on a device that recognizes a person's unique body odor. Tests have shown it to be 85 percent accurate.

TURKEY: *No one knew because they were such good thieves!* Thieves stole an entire 82-foot, 44,000 pound steel bridge that went over a creek in a rural province. No one knows how they were able to dismantle the entire structure without anyone knowing, but they are believed to have taken it to sell for scrap.

TURKEY: A court in Istanbul formally arrested a Ukrainian man who allegedly tried to hijack a turkey bound flight to Sochi, Russia, as the winter Olympics were beginning. The Anadou News Agency reported that the man, AK, was ordered jailed following questioning by police. It was further reported that the man claimed he had a bomb and tried to divert the Pegasus Airlines flight, which originated in Kharkiv, Ukraine. The pilot tricked him and instead landed in Istanbul where he was subdued by officers who had sneaked on board. Ukrainian officials maintain that AK tried to hijack the plane to press for release of anti-government protesters in his country.

ZAMBIA: *Sounds more like they're having wet dreams!* It has been reported that teachers in Zambia are threatening to quit over "invisible witches" sleeping with them at night. The report goes on to maintain that educators in Siavonga have packed their belongings and are ready to flee, claiming "wizards and witches" are forcing them to have sex. "The male teachers complained that they have been having sex with women they cannot see," said traditional leader Chief Sinadambwe, who is calling on the government for help.

THE END

About the Author

Professor Birdsong received his J.D. from the Harvard Law School and his B.A. from Howard University. He teaches law in Orlando, Florida.

After graduation from law school he worked four years at the law firm of Baker Hostetler. He then entered into a varied and distinguished career in government service. He served as a diplomat with the U.S. State Department with various postings in Nigeria, Germany and the Bahamas.

Professor Birdsong later served as a federal prosecutor. After leaving government service, and before he began teaching, Professor Birdsong was in private law practice in Washington, D.C.

www.BirdsongsLaw.com
lbirdsong@barry.edu

Ordering Information

New books coming soon!

Dear Reader,

If you liked this book, I would greatly appreciate you writing me a review on Amazon or any other book site.

I look forward to sharing more funny stories with you in future books.

Thank you, I really appreciate your help.

Regards,

Professor Birdsong

Winghurst Publications
1969 S. Alafaya Trail / Suite 303
Orlando, FL 32828-8732
www.BirdsongsLaw.com
lbirdsong@barry.edu

Other books by
Professor Birdsong:

- Professor Birdsong's 77 Dumbest Criminals Stories (Kindle & Paperback)

- Professor Birdsong's 147 Dumbest Criminal Stories: Florida (Kindle)

- Professor Birdsong's 157 Dumbest Criminal Stories (Kindle & Paperback)

- Professor Birdsong's 177 Dumbest Criminal Stories – International (Kindle & Paperback)

- Professor Birdsong's Weird Criminal Law Stories (Kindle)

- Professor Birdsong's "365" Weird Criminal Law Stories for Every Day of the Year (Kindle)

- Professor Birdsong's Weird Criminal Law Stories, Volume 2: Stories From Around the States and Abroad (Kindle)

- Professor Birdsong's Weird Criminal Law Stories, Volume 3: Stories From New York City and the East Coast. (Kindle)

- Professor Birdsong's Weird Criminal Law Stories - Volume 4: Stories from the Midwest (Kindle)

- Professor Birdsong's Weird Criminal Law Stories, Volume 5: Stories from Way Out West (Kindle)

- Professor Birdsong's Weird Criminal Law Stories - Volume 6: Women in Trouble (Kindle)

- Professor Birdsong's Weird Criminal Law - Volume 6: Women in Trouble! (Paperback)

www.ingramcontent.com/pod-product-compliance
Lightning Source LLC
Chambersburg PA
CBHW021200020426
42331CB00003B/147